I hope this book will be a special reminder of your visit to South Carolina!

Mike Jarrett

ASTHO - 1990
Charleston, S.C.

SOUTH CAROLINA
The Natural Heritage

South Carolina
The Natural Heritage

Photography by Robert C. Clark
Text by Stephen H. Bennett
and Thomas M. Poland

Foreword by James Dickey

Thomas M. Poland
Stephen H. Bennett

Robert C. Clark

University of
South Carolina Press

A portion of the royalties from the sale of this book are being donated to The South Carolina Wildlife and Marine Resources Department's CHECK FOR WILDLIFE FUND.

Copyright © University of South Carolina 1989

Published in Columbia, South Carolina, by the University of South Carolina Press

Manufactured in the United States of America

Designed by Robin A. Sumner

Library of Congress Cataloging-in-Publication Data

Clark, Robert C., 1954–
    South Carolina : the natural heritage / photography by Robert C. Clark ; text by Stephen H. Bennett and Thomas M. Poland ; foreword by James Dickey.
       p.   cm.
    Includes bibliographical references.
    ISBN 0-87249-665-1
    1. Natural history—South Carolina. I. Bennett, Stephen H., 1952– . II. Poland, Thomas M., 1949– . III. Title.
QH105. S6C58 1989
508.757—dc20   89-38185
                                                                            CIP

WE LOVINGLY DEDICATE THIS BOOK TO OUR PARENTS.

In memory of Stephen H. Bennett, Sr.
ꙮ
Elizabeth B. Bennett

Jack H. Clark
Phyllis T. Clark

John M. Poland
Mary Ruth Poland

ACKNOWLEDGMENTS

We gratefully wish to thank the following organizations and individuals for their help and encouragement: The Staff of the Nongame and Heritage Trust Section of the South Carolina Wildlife and Marine Resources Department; Best Photo, Inc.; Sarah Arndt, Veda S. Bennett, Ted Borg, Jay Browne, Tim Burke, Jack and Phyllis Clark, Ben Fortson, Michael Foster, Gail and Ashley Fuller, J. Whitfield Gibbons, Bobby Gladden, Jeffrey Hipp, Bill Mace, Watson McKaskill, Lance and Maria McKinney, David and Ann Merline, Wynn Merline, Paul Nystrom, Janice Sauls, and Tommy Strange.

Contents

Foreword by James Dickey   9

Introduction   13

The Mountain Province   17
The Piedmont   35
The Coastal Plain   53
   The Sandhills   55
    The Upper Coastal Plain   66
   The Coastal Zone   78

Epilogue   94
Photographer's Comments   95
Bibliography   96

❧ Foreword

We are all in danger of becoming outsiders, thrust by our own technology "east of Eden"; displaced persons who can no longer reach in any personal way the colors on the trees, the slow turning of the earth through the seasons. It has been over a hundred years since a poet—George Meredith—could say, "my heart shot into the breast of the bird," and mean it.

And yet there is a return, so long as the world lasts, so long as the plants and creatures hold their life.

For it is life—*life*—they hold—nothing else—these leaves and flowers and creatures, among whom we perpetually find ourselves, exiled in mind as we are. Any time we turn our eyes to the natural world we are moving along that return, and into a kind of personal vision: the world itself as a revelation, and one given only to the living. In our time we must ask ourselves how much of this we are damaging, and ask also whether anything we have created is so beautiful or original as the least aspect of the vision bequeathed to us. Philip Wylie, for example, would have us believe that "the sum total of human works, the artifacts of savages, barbarians, medieval men and modern, all cities and towns, every hut, hovel, skyscraper and temple, all steel bridges, everything man has made to use since the first stone tool or wooden club—does not equal, in all parts put together, the achievements of the life forms of plant and insect in a square foot of grass." Yes; it is true.

What laboratory could make that square foot? Even if the scientists could contrive the grass, it would still be an imitation, strictly second-hand, inferior. Would it not?

During any encounter with a part of the God-created cosmos it is good to remember the word "emergence." If the mind blanks properly and the instincts take over, one will sense something like this happening, as the self drops off and the feeling part of the personality—spirit, what used to be called the soul—enters into union, "like a sudden extension of consciousness," with the thing beheld: the entity small or large, fleeting or permanent, the snowflake or the galaxy, the leaf or the nebula.

South Carolina has its abundant share of these natural visions; all we need to do is to enter into the states of being they make possible: as the naturalist John Hay says, each such state constitutes "a first opening into original space." From the mountains of Oconee to the beaches of Pawleys Island, these kinds of original space exist any time we open ourselves to them, and merely *look* without thought of using: of subdividing, of putting up factories and shopping malls, of mining, of extracting, of gathering, of any kind of exploitation. We need to substitute instinct for reason, and merely to *behold* what is; and view with primal innocence those parts of creation that have nothing to do with us except to serve as material for contemplation and wonder, born into it as we were, living by means of its processes, part of a mystery, part of a whole scheme, a cosmos, the reason for which will never be known. I would like to believe that this book may be for certain human beings the true opening of some of these windows, in our State, into these possible states of existence, as though the reader were being prepared to walk, as he should, bareheaded, openfaced and step-by-step, into a miracle, saying, "It is here. Still. And *I* am here," but returning always to the words, "*It* is here. Still. While I am alive. It is still here."

—*James Dickey*

South Carolina
The Natural Heritage

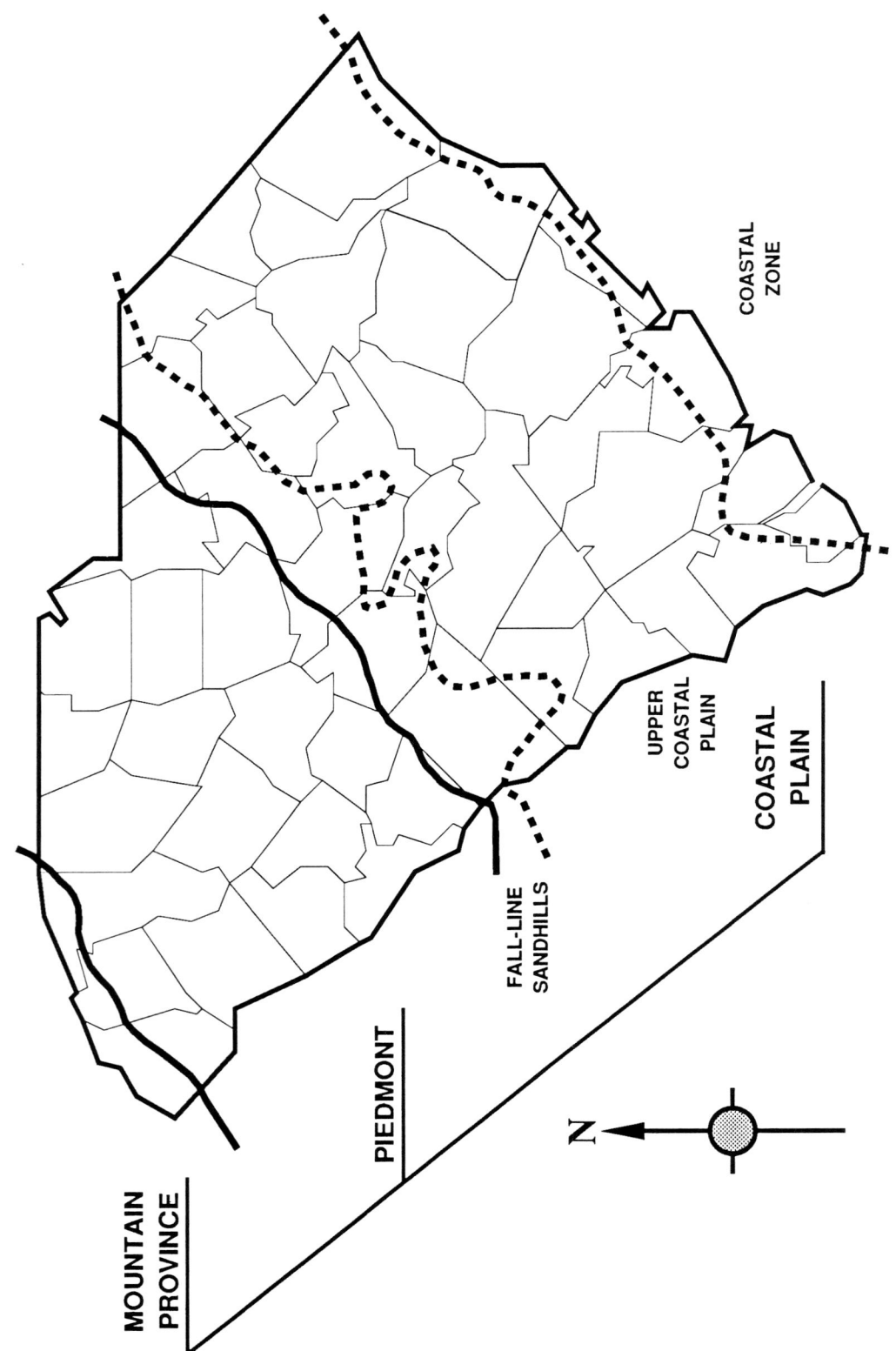

❧ Introduction

With a little over 31,000 square miles, South Carolina is not a large state. It ranks fortieth in land area among the fifty states. But small as it may be, this triangular state plays host to an amazing array of natural habitats.

South Carolina, in fact, can boast a natural diversity one might expect to find in a larger state. Mountains rise up in the northwest corner. The Piedmont sits literally "at the mountain's foot." Coastal plains roll through the inland. Lowlands, swamps and wetlands sprinkle the land with abundant wildlife, and an extensive seashore rounds out a strong geographical personality.

South Carolina lies approximately 32 to 35 degrees north of the equator and 79 to 83 degrees west of Greenwich. Lands at similar latitudes such as Algeria and Syria enjoy nowhere near the diversity of life that flourishes in South Carolina. What accounts for such a richness of life here?

The answer is complex. Unlike many lands, South Carolina lies beneath an unusual overlapping of tropical and temperate zones. This is due in part to such obvious influences as latitude, elevation and continental position, the proximity of the Appalachian Mountains and the Atlantic Ocean.

Climate plays a vital role, and breaking climate down into its components, we find more specific influences: average annual temperatures, precipitation, humidity, hours of sunshine received (solar radiation affects the temperature of the soil's surface, and this affects the amount of moisture in the air), and prevailing winds such as sea breezes.

It all equates to the fact that, for now at least, South Carolina is a relatively temperate land. Its average temperature is approximately 62° Farenheit. Rainfall averages about 48 inches per year, and the precipitation is well-distributed both across the state and through the seasons. Summer receives the heaviest rains; autumn the lightest.

The subtropical climate for which South Carolina is famous is also influenced by the Gulf Stream, the warm ocean current flowing out of the Gulf of Mexico through the straits of Florida and into the Atlantic Ocean not far off the South Carolina coast.

At its most fundamental level, ground level, if you like, the diversity of life can be traced back to geology. The natural character of South Carolina begins with rock which, in turn, is broken down by geologic forces and complemented by organic material to produce soil.

From Precambrian times several hundred million years ago, right up to the present, geological forces have been manufacturing the rocks, soil and sediments of South Carolina. The dynamic processes of erosion and deposition operate today as they did in the beginning, and they influence every living organism in the state from the mountains to the coast.

South Carolina's geology provides both opportunities and constraints on natural habitat. Habitat reflects vegetation types. Vegetation reflects soil types. Soil types reflect geology. However, it is not always such a simple, straightforward formula. Many gray areas exist in the natural history of any given region. Substrate, whether rock, soil, sand or water does not absolutely dictate what grows on the surface. Other complicating factors enter the picture.

This complex formula has put its stamp on South Carolina's basic geologic provinces: the Mountain Province, the Piedmont and the Coastal Plain. These geologic provinces roughly correspond to physiographic provinces of the same name, based primarily on topography. For natural history purposes we have broken the Coastal Plain into three regions: the Sandhills, the Upper Coastal Plain, and the Coastal Zone.

Natural areas cannot be fully appreciated without understanding how they came to be. That is where the geology, geography and climate of South Carolina come in: they hold the key to understanding natural change.

South Carolina is changing right now. Many of the changes will occur at the hands of man. We will not discuss those changes. Nor will our photographs deal with that. Some of the changes affecting South Carolina are part of nature. Plants and animals change over long, long periods of time, and we consider these changes to be evolutionary in nature.

The plant communities discussed in the text change over periods of years. When one community gives away to another community, it is referred to as ecological succession. Some changes in specific habitats occur rapidly. A gust of wind fells a large tree in a forest, and fresh shafts of sunlight immediately invite new plant species to invade the area. The fallen tree is set upon by a host of organisms that break it down . . . live in it . . . consume it, and eventually return it to the earth from which it sprang.

A wind-felled tree is but one of the infinite acts of nature in the long-running play of life. A tree that succumbs to the blade of a bulldozer or the chain of a power saw, well . . . that is another story.

This book portrays various aspects of South Carolina's natural history, a dynamic activity interconnected by all the forms of change we have mentioned. Too much of that which is nature flies right by us. Natural history is somewhat analogous to a film. One frame quickly follows another and another until a whole sequence runs by. The individual frames are lost in the sequence as they blend into what appears to be a normal moving image.

Examine a film sequence frame by frame, and you actually see how small changes in one visual lead to the next image. Study the sequence frame by frame, and you rediscover the mind's ability to perceive motion. Persistence of vision is the key.

One way to comprehend natural history, to see how it works is to freeze it momentarily. Stop the action.

Rediscover the natural world.

South Carolina is a land with a rich natural history, a natural history that never stops changing. South Carolina is a land deserving of a refreshened perception. Persistence of vision, again, is the key.

Enjoy the photographs in this book. In a sense, they are slices of a South Carolina frozen in time for posterity. Treasure them. They are a luxury. Everything changes, but the photographs will not.

The underlying theme of this book, quite simply, is to proffer the idea that though the natural world is dynamic and everchanging, our perception occurs in vignettes, a series of static observations . . . like viewing a film.

We have attempted to capture a natural South Carolina as it existed at a given moment, so that you, the reader, can experience and appreciate the natural workings of a beautiful land called South Carolina frame by frame.

The Mountain Province

Misty Mountain
Mists clad the vales with visible humidity. From the vapors condense droplets which wear down the mountains. Ample water, however, encourages and sustains vegetal growth which retards erosion. Nature's checks and balances at work.
Early morning in June in Oconee County.
F 22, 1/2 Second, 80mm, Fuji 50, 2.25 format

It is raining, again, for the fifth straight day in South Carolina's mountains. That's not unusual at all when you consider that more rain falls in the mountains than in any other part of the state.

Many days the silhouettes of forested ridges burn against a bright blue sky; other days low-hanging clouds obscure the mountains with soft mists. Often rains from a dark sky drench the slopes.

When winter fronts collide, a storm may bring a fantasia of precipitation to the mountains and a crystalline glaze may coat the land, or perhaps the whisper of fluttering snowflakes damp the wooded slopes with a peculiar quiet.

Whether it's a trickle, a torrent, or a winter's snow, abundant precipitation contributes to the uniqueness of the Mountain Province, South Carolina's most rugged terrain.

The Blue Ridge Mountains, that part of the Appalachians cutting across South Carolina's northwestern tip, are extremely ancient. Approximately 350 million years ago, the mountains were forged from sedimentary and igneous rocks squeezed by the pressures of geologic upheaval. The jagged, new-born mountains towered over the land. They were among the tallest mountains in the world.

The resultant crystalline schists and gneisses proved formidable opponents to erosion, but erosion is a persistent, patient, not-to-be-denied process.

Through the millenia, weathering and moving water have worn down the Blue Ridge peaks bit by bit. A steady stream of crystalline schist and gneissic rock particles that were once mountains has long washed seaward as sand.

The ample precipitation and warmer temperatures of the southeastern United States accelerated the effects of weathering and erosion upon the once-jagged peaks. One of the world's oldest mountain chains—ancient compared to the relatively new Rocky Mountains— the Blue Ridge peaks have long endured the diminishing effects of water, gravity, weathering and erosion.

Millions upon millions of years of exposure to the elements have worn the peaks of the Blue Ridge down, round, and smooth like the teeth of a well-used saw.

Today, the approximate 600-square-mile Blue Ridge area contains peaks ranging from 1,400 to 3,500 feet above sea level but rising only 1,000 to 2,000 feet above their valleys. The Blue Ridge Escarpment, the edge of the Blue Ridge Mountains as evidenced by the sheer granitic cliffs of Table Rock, Caesar's Head and numerous waterfalls, dominates much of the province.

❧ BLUE RIDGE VISTA
Blue ridges roll like breakers through the mist. The Blue Ridge is so-named because air molecules scatter the ultraviolet spectrum of sunlight giving the mountains their prevalent blue haze.
LATE AFTERNOON IN MAY IN OCONEE COUNTY. F 16, 1/30 SECOND, 200MM, KODACHROME 64

❧Cove Forest
Lush vegetation could be no more evident. Jade, mint, emerald and other shades of green convey the rich diversity of cove forest vegetation flourishing in the watershed of a nearby creek.
An early afternoon in June in Pickens County. F 22, 1 Second, 55mm, Kodachrome 25

❧Folded Rocks
Convoluted rocks detail the folding and pressure that thrust up the Blue Ridge Mountains. Subtle colors reveal sediment layers deposited aeons ago on some long-lost shore. Metamorphism's intense heat and pressure solidified the sediments providing raw material for mountain-building.
Midafternoon in June near Caesar's Head.
F 16, 1 Second, 55mm, Kodachrome 64

❧Whitewater Falls (facing page)
Lower Whitewater Falls, a series of falls cascading over rocky plateaus, appears to present the classic confrontation: An irresistible force meeting an immovable object. The encounter between rock and water is no contest as running water is the strongest natural force on the planet. Given enough time no rock can withstand its force.
A midafternoon in June in Pickens County.
F 11, 1/60 Second, 105mm Macro, Kodachrome 64

❧Eastatoe Creek

Eastatoe Creek courses through a land of verdant corridors where old-growth hemlock and rare plants such as trillium and Tunbridge fern grow. The self-sustaining trout inhabiting Eastatoe Creek must navigate the rocky stepdowns of a steep gorge, referred to as one of the most tropical areas in North America.

EARLY MORNING IN JUNE IN EASTATOE GORGE. F 22, 1/2 SECOND, 80MM, FUJI 50, 2.25 FORMAT

Despite aeons of weathering and the powerful effect of moving water, the Blue Ridge Mountains display surprising relief. Peaks soar. Many slopes plunge steeply.

Rising above the Piedmont, the mountains intercept moisture-laden clouds blowing in from the west. And because the elevations are higher and the air cooler (average annual temperature is approximately 57° Farenheit), rain condenses more easily there. Thus, the highest average annual rainfall in the state, rainfall ranging from 60 to 80 inches, falls upon our mountains.

It's not surprising that lush cloaks of vegetation veil the mountains.

Rivulets and tiny streams begin as springs atop the peaks, weave into lacy filaments, then cascade seaward, eventually merging and intertwining to produce larger tapestries of water. Ultimately, drops of water that began as rivulets and springs become streams that feed rivers. Coursing through the folds and pleats of the Blue Ridge where green valleys find shelter, rivers downcut an ancient land.

❧Pine Ridge
Though soil thinly covers the granitic rocks, the roots of pine trees penetrate and grip the ridgetop. Maples and other trees also take hold. As the trees annually drop their needles and leaves, organic matter accumulates, giving future trees a better foundation.
Late afternoon in October near Caesar's Head.
F 16, 1/8 Second, 24mm, Kodachrome 25

❧Fallen Oak
A fallen oak set upon by bracken fungi that, in time, will convert the trunk back into raw organic material. Decomposing vegetation is one of the building blocks of soil and, perhaps, one day the nutrients derived from this dead oak will support another tree and, for certain, mountain ferns.
Midmorning in June in Eastatoe Gorge. F 16, 1/4 Second, 55mm Macro, Kodachrome 64

The Mountain Province ❧

PINE-FRINGED GRANITE
Appearances deceive. A common pine-bordered outcropping conceals a rare natural area. Water trickling down the extreme right-hand face of the granite nurtures Mountain sweet pitcher plants and Indian paintbrush, both rare plants. Seepages and unusual habitat sometimes go hand-in-hand, and this is the case here.
MIDMORNING IN MAY IN GREENVILLE COUNTY. F 16, 1/30 SECOND, 55MM, KODACHROME 25

The Chattooga, Whitewater, Thompson, Horsepasture, Toxaway, and Eastatoe rivers receive many of the accumulated rivulets of this region and eventually channel them into the Savannah River drainage system. The Saluda River drains the eastern portion of the province and ultimately flows into the Santee River drainage system.

The rivers, as they always do, carve away at the land, carrying suspended particles of Blue Ridge Mountains seaward. Rivers act as great shapers of the land carrying soil from one area to another. The process is subtle, almost unnoticed, but over the aeons water sculpts the face of the mountains, chiseling and chipping away at the rocks.

The rivers of the Mountain Province speed their clear waters over a topography featuring steplike rocks barely inundated by cascading waters, smoothed by the force of running water. Occasionally, the water level drops to reveal pe-

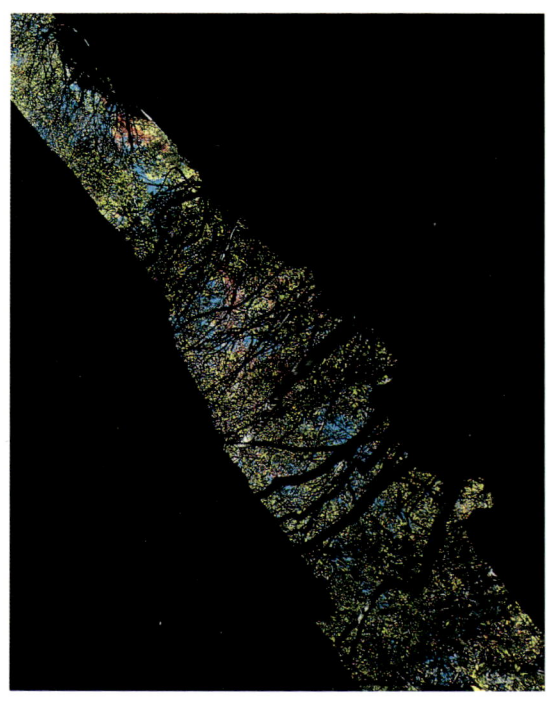

ROCK FRACTURE
A fracture colorfully named the Devil's Kitchen. Seeping into crevices, crystallizing water applys 400 pounds of pressure per square inch against rock walls. Repetitious freezings chip away rock, widening the fissure. Geologic shifting can also open and widen fractures.
LATE AFTERNOON IN OCTOBER IN GREENVILLE COUNTY. F 16, 1/4 SECOND, 24MM, KODACHROME 25

culiar holes where a rock driven by the hydraulic force of running water has drilled into a granite face.

Seepages, moist rocks and glittering waterfalls attest to water's ample presence in the Mountain Province. Abundant water, changing elevation and a host of other natural factors open the possibility for habitat diversity.

Though South Carolina's Blue Ridge Province is small, plentiful flora, fauna and natural habitats exist there. Natural settings sprinkle the state's northwestern corner. And in these scattered locales, remnants of a wild, long-lost land provide glimpses of another time and place. Sheer inaccessibility shelters what's left of ancient habitats, the preponderance of which long-ago disappeared.

The moist seepages and waterslides resulting from the Mountain Province's geology produce unusual habitats. Remnant natural areas such as high-elevation mountain bogs and cataract bogs are rare, but they exist in South Carolina.

Lingering natural areas of the mountains provide settings for bionomic jewels. The mountain sweet pitcher plant grows in the mountains of South Carolina. The Indian paintbrush, another rare plant, flourishes in cataract bogs along with the pitcher plant.

The most important factor in determining habitat differences, of course, is the presence of the one resource so vital to life—water. Organisms living near or in water, generally, can live nowhere else.

Water, sunlight, elevation, humidity and, as we've seen, prevailing winds, combined much like ingredients in a time-tested recipe to bless the mountains with rich assemblages of natural habitat. The degree to which each factor exercises its influence determines to a degree whether a cove forest or a rho-

☙STREAMSIDE OCONEE BELLS
In March, delicate white blooms grace stream margins. The rare Oconee bells, one of the earliest blooming wildflowers in the Blue Ridge, occur in the Mountain Province of South Carolina, North Carolina, and Georgia, but nowhere else in the world. While many other plants have vanished from the Earth's landscape, Oconee bells linger on.
A MARCH AFTERNOON IN PICKENS COUNTY.
F 22, 1 SECOND, 55MM MACRO, KODACHROME 64

dodendron thicket inhabits a particular area in the Blue Ridge Province.

In general, the upper slopes remain driest, even though they receive ample rainfall. Exposure to the wind and sun readily dry out the precipitation. Moreover, the upper slopes often suffer severe erosion; consequently, either poor soil or no soil at all exists to trap and hold moisture. The soils of the Mountain Province lack clay substrates and thus water percolates right through. Besides, water quickly runs off steep slopes. A dry, rocky surface exposed to wind and sun is not the most hospitable environment for most plants.

Despite the harsh environment rocky slopes and faces offer, they are not always barren. Oak, hickory and pine do survive there. Taking root in soil-filled cracks and fissures and islands of soil which accumulate in depressions in the rock, the trees eke out a living on the slopes.

Lichens and rock spikemoss grip the open rock, having adapted to life in this extremely harsh environment. Flowering plants such as dwarf dandelion, coreopsis and goldenrod take hold in sites where organic matter, aided by lichens and spikemoss mats, accumulates.

South-facing slopes, unlike other slopes, are drier mainly because of their longer exposure to the drying rays of the sun. Communities of the ridgetops and slopes present mosaics of oak, hickory and pine. Pines tend to dominate the drier south-facing slopes with oaks and hickories being more prevalent on the moister slopes.

Pitch pine, Virginia pine and shortleaf pine are the dominant pine species. Scarlet oak, chestnut oak, white oak, pignut hickory and mockernut hickory are the dominant hardwood species.

Dogwood, sourwood, persimmon and black locust are common ridgetop understory species, and mountain laurel,

❧RHODODENDRON
A flower synonymous with the mountains: the rhododendron. This moisture-loving member of the azalea family forms dense fens on lower slopes in the cove forest. The petal pattern could serve to aid pollination, the unique yellow-green spots providing a visual cue to insects.
A MORNING IN MAY ALONG THE MIDDLE SALUDA.
F 11, 1/4 SECOND, 105 MM MACRO, KODACHROME 25

❧WHITEWATER RIVER (facing page)
The picturesque Whitewater River subtly carves a channel through the hard metamorphic rocks of the Mountain Province, visibly dropping as it encounters rocks less resistant to erosion.
MIDAFTERNOON IN OCTOBER IN PICKENS COUNTY.
F 22, 1 SECOND, 80MM, FUJI 50, 2.25 FORMAT

The Mountain Province 27

fringe tree, blueberry and huckleberry species make up the shrub layer. Common wildflowers of these communities include galax, spotted wintergreen, loosestrife, and blazing star.

Below the ridgetops, dwell the forests of a moister habitat. The American chestnut forests once occurred here. But in the early part of this century, a fungus known as the Oriental Chestnut Blight vanquished these majestic trees. Today, the interlocking canopies of scarlet oak, tulip poplar, yellow birch, black oak, white oak, white ash, umbrella tree, white pine, and numerous other tree species blanket the slopes.

The moister slopes sustain mountain laurel, rhododendron and sweet shrub. A mountain springtime blazes when wildflowers such as Solomon's seal, False Solomon's seal, violets, foam flower, and jack-in-the-pulpit put on a showy display.

Downslope, cove forests arise around springs and stream runs where rich soils and moist conditions nurture a diverse, profuse community. Spring brings a spectacular show of blooming wildflowers to the cove forest. Trilliums, jack-in-the-pulpit, bloodroot, and the rare Oconee bells found only along stream margins brighten the cove forest.

The dense canopy of tulip poplars, hemlocks, basswood, and occasional beech trees shades the shrubs and sub-canopy trees which grow numerous here. Flame azalea, buckeye, pawpaw, rhododendrons, spicebush and silverbell are a few of the numerous species splashing the otherwise dark cove forests with vivid colors.

As the streams flowing from cove forests lose elevation and widen, the

MOUNTAIN COLOR
What can rival a mountain resplendent with fall color? Dwindling daylight shuts down chlorophyll production, and blazing pigments emerge, the hues, tints and pastels of maples, poplars and other hardwoods.
MIDMORNING IN OCTOBER IN OCONEE COUNTY.
F 16, 1/30 SECOND, 200MM, KODACHROME 64

plant species associated with them change. Alders, birches and sycamore as well as white pine and ash begin to appear. There is, however, no precise spot where one habitat ends and another begins.

The important thing to remember is that, in general, no hard edges delineate the different habitat types proceeding from the ridge tops to the coves and from dry, exposed rocks to flowing streams. Subtle shifts in canopy species hint at what are known as transitional zones. Certain species enjoy wider tol-

❧ Paper Hornet Nest
Few creatures stray far from water for very long. The hornet architects of this paper nest built it over the Toxaway River exploiting a strategic position that provides a nearby source of water and an added measure of security.
A MIDAFTERNOON IN NOVEMBER IN PICKENS COUNTY.
F 11, 1/60 SECOND, 105MM, KODACHROME 64

❧ Barren Granite Slope
A barren granite slope, part of the Blue Ridge Escarpment, overlooks a coniferous piedmont forest. Aeons ago, intruding magma cooled and solidified into granite before reaching the earth's surface. Erosion-exposed granite leaves a desolate environment for plants.
EARLY MORNING IN LATE SEPTEMBER IN PICKENS COUNTY. F 22, 1/8 SECOND, 24MM, KODACHROME 25

erances than others, thus they overlap different habitats.

In many ways, the Mountain Province of South Carolina, like the rest of the state, is a crazy quilt of habitats. Within this quiltwork dwell treasures, the animals and plants that have long contributed to South Carolina's wilderness character.

The animal species of South Carolina's Mountain Province, like the plants, are tied to natural habitat conditions. Black bear are synonymous with the mountains, though they range throughout our state. The thick tangles of rhododendron and fetter-bush offer natural habitat to the black bear still dwelling among the mountain coves.

Some species are very limited in their habitat preferences, such as the green salamander. This species requires rock outcrops, where it can be found hiding in the many crevices and fissures running through the ancient mountain rocks.

The black-bellied salamander depends upon the small, clear streams traversing the mountains, while the mountain dusky salamander prefers to

ꙮSNOW-CAPPED BOULDERS
Snow crowns boulders strewn across the middle Saluda River. Perhaps the most beautiful form of the hydrologic cycle, snow falls three to five times a year in the Mountain Province, enveloping the land in alabaster.
LATE AFTERNOON IN JANUARY IN GREENVILLE COUNTY. F 22, 30 SECONDS, 135MM, FUJI 50, 2.25 FORMAT

30   ꙮ SOUTH CAROLINA: *The Natural Heritage*

❧ SPRING-CLAD SLOPE
A mountain springtime offers soft hues from a palette of delicate blossoms. Bursting forth, the blossoms ready the trees for yet another go at the annual cycle of changing seasons.
LATE AFTERNOON IN APRIL IN GREENVILLE COUNTY. F 11, 1/60 SECOND, 200MM, KODACHROME 64

❧ MOUNTAIN PHLOX
A cloud of phlox covers a mountain cut. This beautiful flower quickly adapts to altered areas. If a heavy mountain rain washes away a hillside, volunteering clusters of violet phlox are almost certain to revegetate the area.
MIDMORNING IN MAY IN PICKENS COUNTY.
F 16, 1/2 SECOND, 55MM, KODACHROME 25

live alongside small streams. Brook trout dwell in the cool, clear, boulder-strewn streams rushing through mountain valleys.

The unique conditions of the Mountain Province have produced habitat-restrictive species that might also be referred to as geographically isolated. Peripheral species such as the milksnake, red squirrel and wood frog live only in the mountains of South Carolina as do the woodlands jumping mouse and the coal skink. This is because their geographic range is tied to the mountains which barely dip into the state.

A peripheral species immortalized by Edgar Allan Poe, the common raven, lives only on the higher slopes where its croaking call resounds through the mountains, especially during the summer months.

The spotted skunk, a species not to be confused with its lowland cousin, the striped skunk, is most common in the mountains, though it is occasionally found in the Piedmont. Spotted skunks dwell in many different mountain habitats, wandering freely from the ridgetops to the coves.

The call of a broad-winged hawk occasionally echoes through the hills and valleys. This large buzzard hawk, a common summer resident of the mountains, is far less common throughout the rest of the state.

The black-throated green warbler, black-throated blue warbler, chestnut warbler, solitary vireo, and least flycatcher are small, migratory songbirds which can only be found in South Carolina during their summer stay in the mountains.

The complete list of wildlife to be found in the mountains is a long one.

Some species living there range throughout the state while others are restricted to the mountains, an area with more room than is apparent.

To grasp the true surface area of the Mountain Province, stretch a towel flat on a table top. Then crumple the towel by pushing from each end to simulate the upthrusting of mountains.

Now imagine the extent of the Mountain Province were its peaks and valleys to be stretched flat like a towel. The acreage of this geographic area would, of course, be much larger. So though the Mountain Province actually makes up about two percent of South Carolina's surface area, there is more room for wildlife and its habitat than readily perceived.

The Mountain Province presents many moods: The solitude of a wind-blown ridge, the Piedmont rolling to the horizon, the refreshing energy of a clear stream rushing through a verdant cove forest, the mysterious movement and calling of forest creatures, the roar of white water carving and etching the face of the mountains, the end of another day as a late afternoon sun dips behind forest-clad peaks.

It is all in the Mountain Province, nature's legacy to the land known as South Carolina.

❧River Rocks
Water sculpts the land, polishes boulders and transports particles of mountains seaward. Rushing water is the master architect of geography and an inseparable part of the mountains.
A June twilight on the Middle Saluda River.
F 22, 20 Seconds, 200mm, Kodachrome 64

❧ The Piedmont

Rain is falling across the mountains and foothills of South Carolina's Piedmont. Along plateaus and flat areas, water lingers, but elsewhere rain-fed rivulets are gathering downstream momentum.

Tributaries join force and, soon, sheets of water sweep over the Piedmont.

A land awash swells the upper reaches of rivers.

Repercussions of rain will soon be felt.

Downstream, rivers are peacefully threading their way through gentle valleys separated by the broad uplands of a rolling land. In the low-lying bottoms, herbs and grasses carpet the earth in green. Willow oak, musclewood, sycamore and shagbark hickory sprout in the wetter areas. Understory shrubs—pawpaw, bladdernut, box elder, and strawberry bush—create thickets of cover for small species of wildlife. Box turtles creep along the forest floor. Deer browse.

But the cumulative effect of raindrops will soon change all this.

Waters will rise, and great loads of silt and sediment will soon flow seaward. The rivers will depart the steeper flanks of their banks, and pour into floodplain bottomlands. Wildlife species will take cover . . . head for higher ground. Surging waters will sweep away less mobile members of the community. The ebb

❧ Fall Color
Autumn's blush of red maple plays counterpoint to the yellows of sugar maple on a Piedmont hillside. Red maple occurs throughout South Carolina while sugar maple is more frequently associated with the mountains and Piedmont.
Midafternoon in October in Newberry County.
F 16, 1 Second, 55mm, Kodachrome 64

☙ BILLOWING CLOUDS
Billowing, turbulent clouds foretell the coming of a thunderstorm as a summer cold front pushes a stagnant Bermuda High out to sea. The crisp, clean air will soon darken with rain that will wash even more Piedmont soil into waiting rivers.
LATE AFTERNOON IN AUGUST IN LEXINGTON COUNTY. F 11, 1/125 SECOND, 105MM, KODACHROME 25

and flow of floodwater will draw parallel lines upon buttressed trunks.

When it's all over . . . when the floodwaters subside . . . another layer of fertile sediment will have settled onto the floodplain to sustain the rich life bordering Piedmont rivers. Soil that not so long ago belonged upstream will nourish tulip poplar, sweetgum, and red maple. Life will be richer in the alluvial soils along major stream courses.

South Carolina's Piedmont is a pleasant, rolling land crisscrossed by streams and rivers. A land where gentle slopes unfurl from horizon to horizon. . . a land ever so gradually losing elevation as it sweeps toward the Fall Line. At one end, nearest the Blue Ridge Province, the Piedmont may reach over 1,000 feet. About a hundred miles away, elevations reach 300 feet near the edge of the Sandhills.

Rolling hills, grading from ridgetops to river valleys typify the landscape features of the Piedmont, a land residing upon layered rocks consisting of thick strata resting upon an ancient metamorphic rock assemblage known as the "basement complex." The basement complex lies concealed in the South Carolina Piedmont, though it crops up in the westernmost part of the South Carolina Blue Ridge along the Chattooga River.

A curious landform distinguishes the rolling terrain of the Piedmont: the monadnock. The elevated summits of monadnocks remain above the surrounding land where vulnerable areas have long been washed away by millenia of erosion.

These small, isolated mountains are

❧Buttressed Trees
Greenery springs up along the Little River in an area recently vacated by water. A twisted, buttressed trunk framed by the luxuriant growth of violets and other herbs attest to the rigors—and richness—of life in the dynamic floodplain habitat.
Midafternoon in April in Fairfield County.
F 22, 1/15 Second, 50mm, Fuji 50, 2.25 Format

residual features generally consisting of rocks more resistant to weathering than the surrounding rocks. Often, monadnocks are granite. As the surrounding, "softer" rocks erode and wash away, the more resistant rocks ever so gradually become more exposed. Eventually, they enjoy superior elevation over the surrounding land. Most monadnocks in South Carolina occur within twenty miles of the Blue Ridge.

With hills and monadnocks looming above the terrain, the Piedmont, like the Blue Ridge, displays an ancient geologic history. The province's metamorphic basement rock—slates, schists, gneisses, diabase, gabbro and granitic intrusions—ranges from 1 to 1.3 billion years old. Folded and faulted, these crystalline rocks closely resemble those of the Blue Ridge.

Geologic change creeps along, a slow, tedious process, but it accounts for dramatic changes on the face of the Earth. Approximately 600 million years ago, an island lay off the coast of the early North American continent.

That island would someday be known as the Piedmont.

The land mass collision forcing up the Blue Ridge Mountains about 470 million years ago drove that ancient island into North America. Continental drift continued and a then-new North America crashed into northwest Africa, creating the ancient supercontinent known as Pangaea. What would be the Piedmont absorbed the impact of the colliding continents.

Over an immense period of time, the rebounding continents drifted to their present locations, assuming an identity similar to that recognized today.

Geologic change, of course, never stopped affecting the Piedmont. Streams have been cutting across this region for millions of years, removing material and carving the land into the forms present today.

Today, the Piedmont is a region known for rolling topography and, with annual rains of 45 to 60 inches falling upon it, great watersheds. Rolling relief, basement bedrock, clay-rich soils and ample mountain precipitation contribute to the Piedmont's character as a great shedder of water. Water runs along

ATAMASCO LILIES
A spray of white Atamasco lilies graces the Little River floodplain. Known also as the Easter Lily because of the time of its bloom, it is one of the few spectacular wildflowers inhabiting the dynamic floodplain habitat.
LATE AFTERNOON IN APRIL IN FAIRFIELD COUNTY.
F 16, 1/15 SECOND, 55MM, KODACHROME 25

❧Foggy River Birch
A cloak of white shrouds river birch, cottonwoods and sycamore and muffles the tumbling Saluda River's descent over an outcropping of fall line rock. The Fall Line separates the Piedmont from the Coastal Plain and is most prominent at rocky sites where rivers lose their greatest amount of elevation over the shortest distance.
Early morning in January in Richland County.
F 16, 1/30 Second, 105mm, Kodachrome 64

❧Fence Lizard
Blink and you might miss this fence lizard poised on the trunk of a small oak tree. Called fence swifts by some, these small, arboreal lizards match their habitat, a trait helping them capture small insects and spiders as well as minimizing detection by their own predators.
Sunrise in September in Lexington County.
F 16, 1/8 Second, 105mm, Kodachrome 25

❧Jagged Lightning
Lightning traces a dendritic pattern through the cool spring atmosphere, and jagged bursts of color shred the evening sky. Uncontrolled wildfires sparked by lightning once burned openings into forests thus influencing many of South Carolina's natural habitats.
Evening in early May in Richland County.   F 4, Open Shutter, 35mm, Kodachrome 25

the surface where dense clay soils resist percolation.

Erosion has long plagued the Piedmont. Rivers like the Saluda, Broad, Savannah, and Catawba not only carry great loads of water, they transport great quantities of topsoil. Rain leaches nutrients and other minerals from topsoil leaving insoluble iron and clays behind, imparting characteristic colors to the upper layers of the soil—colors that often carry over to the rivers running through them. The Pee Dee carries clayey silt and appears to be red. . . . The Enoree runs yellow.

Fertile floodplains stretch out along the large rivers dominating the Piedmont, and heavy precipitation periodically floods the flat, low-lying river valleys. These dynamic habitats regularly receive fresh layers of silt, so bottomland hardwood forests grow rich and thick. But, they must sustain flood damage on a nearly predictable basis.

Depending on the floodplain's width and surrounding forest type, the tree species of floodplain forests vary. The time of flooding and its duration influence forest composition as well.

For the most part, sweetgum, tulip poplar, winged elm, red maple and river birch dominate the floodplain forest. A tangled understory of shrubs may feature pawpaw, bladdernut, box elder, and strawberry bush.

Vines hang from the canopy where they have crept up throughout the floodplain forest creating skeins that may include wild yam, cat brier, green brier, trumpet vine, Virginia creeper, wild grape and virgin's bower. The herbaceous or wildflower layer lies depauperate due to the physical dynamics of the forest—buffeting by floodwaters—the dense shade of the forest canopy.

In some cases, tree and shrub species associated with larger river's floodplains grow along the small streams and rivers running throughout the Piedmont. Buttonbush, black willow and alder, and in some cases meadows of sedges and bulrushes grow thick and green.

As in the mountains, the water avail-

❧ Enoree Sunrise
When warm August air and cool river waters interface, condensing moisture shrouds the Enoree with the vapors of dawn, obscuring sunrise.
Sunrise in August in Laurens County.   F 5.6, 1/60 Second, 55mm, Kodachrome 64

❧Crimson Samaras
Crimson samaras, the winged fruit of red maple, overhang the Little River. When the time is right, they will helicopter air currents to the river . . . wash downstream and complete the age-old ritual of dispersal.
Early afternoon in April in Union County.   F 5.6, 1/60 Second, 55mm, Kodachrome 64

❧Snow-White Blossoms
Dogwood's white blossoms fleck the green monochrome of newly leafed-out hardwoods on a hillside. The blossoms will last but a while; the leaves will work all spring and summer until fall puts them to rest.
Late afternoon in early April in Lancaster County.   F 16, 1/8 Second, 55mm, Kodachrome 25

ॐ Jeweled Web
Strung on silk, dewdrops mimic glass beads and tiny jewels as they capture and reflect autumn's morning light along the concentric circles of a spiderweb.
Early morning in October in Lexington County.   F 16, 1/30 Second, 105mm, Kodachrome 64

❧ Meadow of Flowers

Black-eyed Susans and white-flowered goldenrod blanket an unusual glade, a remnant, perhaps, of once widespread prairie habitat. Ideally suited to the wildflowers, the glade's Iredell soil results when weathering breaks down basic parent rock, producing earth circumneutral in nature.

Late afternoon in mid-September in York County.   F 22, 1/8 Second, 35mm, Kodachrome 25

🌿Spider Lilies
Rocky Shoal spider lilies in the splendor of full bloom grow amid the polished stones of a Catawba River shoal. These rare plants are restricted to rocky shoals . . . unique habitats found only in Piedmont streams and rivers.
Early morning in June in Chester County. F 22, 1/15 Second, 35mm, Kodachrome 25

able in the soil determines to a large degree the presence of vegetation. Higher elevations tend to be drier—lower areas wetter. Piedmont ridgetops, for instance, are drier while the river valleys run moist and humid. The driest ridgetop forests are those exposed to the most sunlight, i.e., south- or southwest-facing and lying on thin soils.

The native pine dominating these ridgetops is the shortleaf pine. Blackjack oak and post oak generally dominate the oak species of these drier forests. White oak, red oaks, persimmon and mockernut hickory also grow in this habitat type. In general, the moister a particular site, the greater the diversity of tree species.

North-facing slopes, the Piedmont's moister upland slopes, support oak-hickory forests with a number of canopy and subcanopy species. The roll call of common species along these slopes is a long one: blackgum, black oak, dogwood, shagbark hickory, loblolly pine, mockernut hickory, red maple, red oak, chestnut oak, scarlet oak, short-leaf pine, sourwood, southern red oak, tulip poplar and white oak.

The chemical nature of the soil on upland and downslope Piedmont sites can cause a shift in the forest type. Chestnut oaks reign in the forests generally growing on acidic north-facing slopes. This particular forest type was once dominated by American chestnut which now occurs only as stump sprouts. Mountain laurel and buffalo nut can be found in this forest type. Herbaceous growth is generally sparse.

On sheltered, north-facing slopes where the soil is either circumneutral, i.e., almost neutral or basic, a somewhat different forest prevails. Joining previously mentioned tree species are Shumard's oak, red buckeye, sugar maple and beech trees. These mixed-hardwood forests may support such wildlflowers as pink lady slipper orchid, an orchid known as downy rattlesnake plantain, cranefly orchid, and spotted wintergreen.

Wildflowers and the Piedmont's "basic" forests go hand-in-hand. Flowering species are particularly diverse in this unusual habitat. Anemone, trilliums, bloodroot, liverleaf, adder's tongue,

❧Edge of a Flatrock
Sandwort, mule's ear, and diamorpha find ample soil and sunlight along the edge of a flatrock where dry woods and red cedars abut bare granite.
Late afternoon in April in Lancaster County.
F 22, 1/2 Second, 55mm, Kodachrome 25

green violet, bellwort and dwarf iris are commonly found. Rare or uncommon plant species can also be discovered. Wild ginger, moonseed, isopyrum, Carolina larkspur, ginseng and broadleaf coreopsis are among the rarities associated with these forests. The basic forest, unusual in South Carolina, is associated with weathering "parent" rock which forms the basic soil.

Varieties of the above forest types, except for those along the ridgetops, can be found in Piedmont coves. Like mountain cove forests, Piedmont cove forests tend to be moist and cool and

SLATE-COLORED JUNCO
Perched among the red berries of deciduous holly, a slate-colored junco scans a nearby hedgerow. Perhaps this sparrow relative is spending a November day in Chester County before migrating south for the winter.
MIDAFTERNOON IN NOVEMBER IN CHESTER COUNTY. F 5.6, 1/250 SECOND, 400MM, KODACHROME 64, FROM A BLIND.

generally found on north or northwest facing slopes. Bitternut hickory, white oak, hop hornbeam, slippery elm, wild azaleas and cucumber tree also dwell in cove forests. Shrubs found there include pawpaw, spicebush and sweetshrub. Trout lily, fly-poison, blazing star, Solomon's seal and false Solomon's seal commonly grow as do heartleaf, spring beauty, wood sorrel, wild geranium and may apple.

From cove forests to granitic outcroppings, life in the Piedmont runs a gamut of habitat conditions. Several habitats within this gamut command special attention. Two relate to particular soil series found in South Carolina only in the upper Piedmont, Iredell and Elbert soils. The dry montmorillonite forest occurs on upland slopes or flat areas over basic rocks, and the wet upland depression swamp forest occurs on poorly drained upland flats. These related forests, one dry, the other wet, are unique habitats in our state and have several rare or uncommon species associated with them. Wild hyacinth is associated with the swamp forest and prairie rosin weed, grey-headed coneflower and Schweinitz's sunflower with the montmorillonite forest.

Rocky shoals in Piedmont rivers are unique habitats associated with exposed rocks in the river bed. The rivers are generally shallow at shoal areas and quite turbulent. Water tumbles through the riffles and smashes against the rocks. Encounters between rock and river mix the water with the atmosphere and high levels of oxygen enrich the water. Aquatic life is abundant here. Invertebrates live beneath the bottoms of river rocks. Caddisfly and other insect larvae dwell among the shoals and life runs picturesque here. The rocky shoals spider lily, a rare plant species found only in this habitat, splashes the shoals with sprays of white flowers.

Granitic domes and flatrocks are both outcroppings of granite, exposed and somewhat bare. Granite flatrocks are extruded or exposed granite generally level with the surrounding landscape. The communities present on both features are similar, but flatrocks are much more diverse in flora, more uncommon and have a number of rare and endemic species associated with them.

❧May Apple and Trilliums
May apples, trilliums, isopyrum, sweet cicely, and spring beauty.... The circumneutral soil at the base of a bluff overlooking a Piedmont stream grows a bounty of wildflowers in a habitat of basic forest.
Early morning in April in McCormick County. F 22, 1 Second, 80mm, Fuji 50, 2.25 Format

Buckeye Butterfly
The bright colors of a buckeye butterfly contrast sharply with the yellow flowers of sneezeweed. Easily identified by the large eyespots of the upper wing, the buckeye is common throughout the state. Caterpillars of this butterfly feed primarily on plantain, gerardia, false loosestrife and toadflax.
Late afternoon in September in Lexington County. F 11, 1/30 Second, 105mm, Kodachrome 64

Solution pools, caused through the chemical solutioning of the rock by rainwater are unique microhabits found on granite flatrocks. These somewhat circular pools fill with two to three inches of water during the winter months and dry to bare, thin soil (in some cases) during the summer months. The pool's size and depth and the deepness of the soil accumulation determine the plants to be found. Pool sprite, quillwort, sandwort, Puck's orpine, and diamorpha are all rarities associated with solution pools at different successional stages.

Elsewhere on the rock, mosses and lichens may occur in exposed areas and pines and cedars may grow in soil accumulated in cracks and fissures and large, old solution pools.

It is an age-old story—regardless of

the conditions—even upon the cold face of granite, organisms have evolved and adapted to live there . . . to fill niches. Life in the Piedmont mirrors the history of life throughout the world.

And so, the distinctive natural areas of the Piedmont feature a richly diverse assemblage of plant and animal life. Numerous unusual plants and plant communities are restricted to the Piedmont, but the wildlife species are less confined.

Save for exceptions such as the Webster's salamander which occurs in South Carolina only in the Piedmont along the Savannah River, the vast majority of Piedmont species are more cosmopolitan. The Piedmont, shares many species with both the Mountain Province and the Coast.

The red fox, though it occurs in both the Coastal Plain and the Piedmont, is more frequently encountered in the Piedmont.

The swamp rabbit, a relative of the cottontail, occurs in both the western Mountains and Piedmont where it inhabits floodplains, canebrakes and wet areas.

Other Piedmont animals come and go on a seasonal basis. The whip-poor-will spends summers in the Mountains and the Piedmont, but resides in the Coastal Plain during the winter. (Thus no calls can be heard from the whip-poor-will in the Piedmont winter.)

On the other hand, the black-and-white warbler breeds in the Mountains and the Piedmont during the summer, but winters all over the state. The painted turtle suns along the backwaters of river marshes. Most common in the Piedmont, it is absent from all but the Upper Coastal Plain.

The queen snake prefers small wooded streams of the Mountains and the Piedmont. It, too, is absent from all but the uppermost Coastal Plain.

The eastern chipmunk, a small ground-dwelling squirrel of deciduous woodlands, lives in the Mountains and the Piedmont. Many species find the Piedmont a convenient bridge across the natural vistas of South Carolina.

Perhaps the mobility and pervasiveness of wildlife species attest to the particular place of the Piedmont in South Carolina's natural landscape.

It is the land in between.

What began as an island off the coast of prototypal North America is now a bridge between the ancient North American landmass and the new land lain down by aeons of deposition and ocean retreat.

The Piedmont's special places: the monadnocks, the flatrocks, streams with rocky shoals, the lush floodplains and basic forests brimming with bouquets of wildflowers endow the land at the foot of the mountains . . . the land in between . . . with natural beauty and enchantment.

YELLOW AND BLACK ARGIOPE
A yellow and black argiope, also called the writing spider for its habit of weaving zigzag designs in its web, surveys a silk-enshrouded grasshopper. A struggling prey's vibrations summon the spider which quickly administers venom and wraps the prey in silk.
EARLY MORNING IN SEPTEMBER IN YORK COUNTY.
F 16, 1 SECOND, 105MM, KODACHROME 25

The Coastal Plain

Though the glaciers never came close, ice profoundly affected South Carolina's Coastal Plain.

When global climatic change ushered in the Ice Age, glaciers grew in the north denying the oceans water, and sea levels dropped. Continental glaciers unleashed a stunning change upon the land as the edge of the sea retreated far beyond where it is today. Forsaken shorelines, dunes and deltas lingered, haunting apparitions of a long-lost sea.

Then, melting glaciers freed water to return to the hydrologic cycle. Rain and runoff filled the seas, and the surf rolled in. A resurgent sea covered the Coastal Plains much farther inland than today.

Rivers pouring into the primordial sea above what would be the Coastal Plain dropped silt loads that settled to the ocean's bottom. Dunes arose. For a geologic moment, the sea wavered not.

Then the Ice Age turned fickle. Glacial growth and subsequent melting raked the edge of the sea across South Carolina time and time again, stranding ancient shorelines. Resolute for a time, then responding to glacial melt or formation, an ever-changing surfline pounded crystalline rocks into sand across the breadth of the Coastal Plain.

Then, between ten and fifty thousand years ago, the seas' most recent recession began. Terraces pushed up by Pleistocene shorelines trace the seas' retreat, and to this day an ancient sea bottom stretches across a major portion of the Carolina landscape.

Sandstone Column
A sandstone pillar wearing a cap of erosion-resistant ironstone rises out of a hillside along what was likely an ancient stream valley. Where primeval fish once swam, the scarlet leaves of turkey oak now grow.
Early morning in November in Lexington County. F 16, 1/15 Second, 55mm, Kodachrome 25

Ice did, indeed, profoundly affect South Carolina's Coastal Plain.

The Coastal Plain is, by far, South Carolina's largest and most diverse physiographic province. Bounded on one side by the Fall Line and the Atlantic on another, the Coastal Plain Province encompasses nearly 20,000 square miles, about 66 percent of South Carolina's land area.

Compared to the geologic history of other provinces, the Coastal Plain is a simple land. Unlike the Mountain and Piedmont Provinces, scant rock exists in the Coastal Plain. Limestone or sandstone exists in some areas, but for the most part, these are uncommon.

Layers of silt, sand and marine deposits that settled out of the sea comprise the Coastal Plain. Down deep, beneath the sedimentary layers, a base of crystalline rocks plunges coastward at a harsh angle. Thus, sediments near the Fall Line run a few feet thin. Near the coastline the sediment layers extend more than 3,000 feet deep.

Rolling from the uplands to a flat stop at the coast, ranging from 300 feet to sea level, the Coastal Plain falls into three subregions: The Fall Line Sandhills, the Upper Coastal Plain and the Coastal Zone. Each region possesses a singular identity. Each leaves an exceptional natural legacy to South Carolina.

Long-leaf pine are resistant to fire and flourish in the Sandhills' dry areas which have long been exposed to lightning's wildfires. Carolina Bays, those mysterious elliptical, oriented depressions, enrich the Upper Coastal Plain. The Coastal Zone boasts fertile salt marshes where spartina supports the sea's food chain.

The Coastal Plain truly possesses that natural character long associated with South Carolina. The dark recesses of swamps, dunes long-abandoned by ancient rivers, pinelands, tannin-stained, tea-colored rivers, a majestic sweep of coast, and sun-splashed barrier islands.

It is all in the Coastal Plain, and it begins with the Sandhills.

᛫RESSURRECTION FERNS
Ressurrection ferns sprout from a sandstone boulder. A reviving rain shower quickly restores verdancy to the drought-induced dormant ferns more typically associated with the stately live oaks of the coast.
EARLY MORNING IN MAY IN LEXINGTON COUNTY.
F 16, 1/15 SECOND, 55MM, KODACHROME 25

THE FALL LINE SANDHILLS

The Sandhills piled across South Carolina present rolling vistas of long-leaf pine, sand covered by reindeer moss and British soldier, exposed sand and sandstone outcrops, but also pockets of rare habitat. The Fall Line Sandhills stretch southwest to northeast from Georgia to North Carolina cutting an irregular swath across the state.

These large deposits of well-drained sand are not dunes left by the receding Pleistocene seas. More likely, the Sandhills are depositional features laid down by streams and rivers. Disintegrating, eroded Piedmont rocks provided much of the sand and clay sediments of the Sandhills.

Gentle slopes and round summits distinguish the Sandhills. Some mounds rise 600 feet above sea level.

Only about 45 inches of precipitation falls upon the Sandhills annually. Consequently, the arid tops and upper slopes produce inhospitable environments, where only species adapted to xeric habitats live, plants and animals adept at moisture conservation.

Long-leaf pines dominate the slopes of the Sandhills; turkey oaks grow throughout the subcanopy. Shrubs associated with these dry forests are huckleberries, blueberries, rosemary, and sparkleberry. Sandwort, prickly pear cactus and ipecac are common herbs. Some rarities associated with these habitats include Georgia bear grass, pine-needle golden aster and woody goldenrod.

Plants employ adaptions enabling

☙Solitary Long-Leaf
A stately long-leaf, the signature pine of the Sandhills, sheds wintry sunlight. These hardy pines not only tolerate drought but also show amazing resistance to fires that occasionally sweep their dry habitat.
Early morning in November in Chesterfield County.   F 22, 1/60 Second, 50mm, Fuji 50, 2.25 Format

them to survive in the near desertlike conditions of the Sandhills. One survival strategy in the Sandhills is succulence, the ability to store water until it's needed, perhaps in a tap root. Another strategy is tortifolia—reorienting leaves so that they absorb less heat and light, and consequently remain moister.

Sandhills and their dry forest communities occur in other places throughout the Coastal Plain, along the fluvial sand deposits of rivers and the sand rims of Carolina Bays.

In the summer months, shimmering waves of heat ripple off the arid tops of sandhills. Raindrops landing there quickly evaporate. Water managing to soak through the coarse sands quickly trickles downslope. The peaks of the Sandhills run bone-dry. Plants find the sandhills to be harsh, unyielding environments. But beneath the dry hills, springs or seeps often occur.

Seeps exist as isolated bogs or more often stream headwaters. Streamhead pocosins, hillside shrub bogs and seepage pocosins are somewhat dominated by thick, shrubby vegetation with varying degrees of openness. On moist, acidic slopes, blueberries, huckleberries, dog-hobble, fetterbushes and cat briers tangle. Aside from the expected plant communities, some extraordinary plants dwell in seepages receiving full sun, the carnivorous pitcher plants and the sundews.

As seeps grow into small streams braiding the Sandhills, two general community types accompany them. One is the Atlantic white cedar bog, an uncommon community so-named because

PITTED IRONSTONE
Rust-colored ironstone lies beneath the green lichens blanketing its pitted surface. Over time, lichen secretions slowly crumble ironstone, a resistant rock often found capping a sandstone outcrop in the sandhills.
MIDAFTERNOON IN EARLY MAY IN LEXINGTON COUNTY. F 16, 1/15 SECOND, 55MM, KODACHROME 25

☙Dead Snag in Pines
"Ghost of the pine forest . . ." a twisted pine remnant hangs in the ephemeral fog drifting through a stand of long-leaf pine upon a sandstone monadnock.
Early morning in May in Chesterfield County.   F 16, 1 Second, 105mm, Kodachrome 64

Pine Barrens Tree Frog
Isolated bogs in the northern Sandhills present the Pine Barrens tree frog with a breeding habitat. It begins when rainfall soaks through the Sandhills to clay. Eventually an outcropping may produce a seepage sustaining shrubs and herbs where this rare amphibian can breed if conditions are right.
Early morning in June in Chesterfield County. F 5.6, 1/125 Second, 105mm, Kodachrome 64

Sundews
The insectivorous sundew's spathelike leaves, borne on rosettes of red-green stalks, perform three different functions. Nectar glands on the leaf surface attract prey. Long-stalked glands above the leaf surface entangle and trap unsuspecting insects. The sundew's leaves then curl about the prey and perform the digestive process.
Late afternoon in August in Lexington County. F 22, 15 Seconds, 105mm with 81c filter, Kodachrome 25

Atlantic white cedar dominates its vegetation. Periodic fires maintain these cedar bogs by preventing plant succession. In fire's absence, however, succession often leads to a more common community, the bay forest, which is dominated by loblolly bay, red bay and Virginia or sweet bay.

Two river types drain the Sandhills. From the Mountains or upper Piedmont flow the meandering brown-water streams, replete with heavy silt washing in from soils of the Piedmont. The Savannah, Broad, Catawba and Great Pee Dee push through, draining great portions of the Coastal Plain.

The other river—the blackwater stream—is most picturesque. These

ICICLES
An Arctic air mass moves south and a January freeze catches water seeping over a sandstone rock formation. Prisms of light within the icicles reflect the subtle earth tones of the rock from which they grow . . . drip by drip.
EARLY MORNING IN JANUARY IN LEXINGTON COUNTY. F 22, 1/60 SECOND, 80MM, FUJI 50, 2.25 FORMAT

60 ❧ SOUTH CAROLINA: *The Natural Heritage*

Pitcher Plants

Purple Pitcher plants . . . death traps in sphagum moss. Nectar glands along the hood and lip lure insects seeking food. Angled filaments then direct curious insects into the pitcher, but prevent departure. An enzyme broth at the pitcher's bottom digests trapped insects, releasing nutrients which the plant absorbs.

MIDAFTERNOON IN LATE AUGUST IN LEXINGTON COUNTY. F 22, 8 SECONDS, 105MM WITH 81C FILTER, KODACHROME 25

quaint rivers generally run smaller than brownwater streams. Originating in the Sandhills as seepages, they carry little silt, though decomposing vegetations' tea-colored tannins saturate them, thus their colorful name. Blackwater streams such as the Edisto, Black and Little Pee Dee drain across the Coastal Plain or feed larger brownwater rivers.

The rivers carry that resource elemental to life, and whether blackwater or brownwater, Sandhill rivers

❧LONG-LEAF PINE CONE
Overhead light skims the tips of a longleaf pine cone producing shadows and highlights that reveal nature's repetitious geometry.
MIDAFTERNOON IN APRIL IN CHESTERFIELD COUNTY. F 16, 1/30 SECOND, 105MM, KODACHROME 25

❧PRICKLY PEAR IN BLOOM
Like the deserts in the western U.S., the Sandhills—the "eastern desert"—is a region of great diversity. It comes alive with plants adapted to extremely arid habitats. Here, vibrant yellow flowers appear out of place atop the spiny pads of prickly pear cactus.
AFTERNOON IN EARLY MAY IN LEXINGTON COUNTY. F 11, 1/15 SECOND, 105MM, KODACHROME 25

❧YELLOW PITCHER PLANTS (facing page)
Yellow pitcher plants, or trumpets, cluster above a white cedar bog's dark, acidic waters. Impoverished of soil nutrients, acidic habitats may have figured in the evolution of insectivory among some plant families.
MORNING IN JUNE IN LEXINGTON COUNTY. F 22, 8 SECONDS, 35MM WITH 81C FILTER, KODACHROME 25

❧Cottontail
Shrubs and grasses (food and cover) surround an eastern cottontail frozen at woods edge. Not far away lies a trail. Startled cottontails usually flee down a well-known trail, giving them an edge over would-be predators.
Early morning in May in Chesterfield County. F 4, 1/250 Second, 105mm, Kodachrome 25, from a blind.

course through the "eastern desert," a land rich with life and subsequent struggles for survival despite its sobriquet.

Red-cockaded woodpeckers chisel cavities facing south in living long-leaf pines so that sunlight can warm and spread the resin oozing down the tree.

Pine Snake
This pine snake's flickering tongue picks up scent molecules in the air and transfers them to the Jacobsen's organ, a specialized structure in the roof of the mouth connected to the olfactory nerve.
Early morning in June in Aiken County. F 5.6, 1/500 Second, 105mm, Kodachrome 25

Resin thwarts tree-climbing snakes that would prey on woodpecker hatchlings. Irritating the sensitive stomach skin, the annoying resin causes snakes to release their grip and fall to the sandy soil before attaining the nest cavity.

Pine barren treefrogs, rare amphibians, breed in small ponds of acidic water. This beautiful species' survival depends on a combination of factors: seepages that support evergreen bogs and periodic fires that prevent plant sucession from altering the bogs' character.

Insects finding the lure of nectar too tempting spend their last Sandhills' day inside a pitcher plant or stuck to a sundew.

Pine snakes and hognose snakes find refuge in stumpholes to escape the searing heat of the Sandhills' sun. Like all reptiles, they must rely on cool shelters to regulate their body temperature or they will perish.

Vignettes of nature abound in the Sandhills, yet another gradation of habitat, life and natural history in that continuum stretching from the Mountains, through the Piedmont to the Coast known as South Carolina.

❧Moss-Draped Cypress
Spanish moss, an air plant, drapes pond cypress trees rising from the black waters of a Carolina Bay. Though these elliptical wetlands dot the Atlantic coastal plain, they tend to concentrate in the Carolinas.
Early morning in May in Sumter County.
F 22, 1/15 Second, 35mm with Polarizing Filter, Kodachrome 25

The Upper Coastal Plain

Rivers traveling through the Upper Coastal Plain will never again flow across metamorphic rocks like those of the Piedmont, at least not for a geologic eternity.

Instead, the rivers spread through the Upper Coastal Plain, a land of sandy sediments fashioned by stream erosion and to some extent wind. Broad and flat for the most part, elevations in the region vary from 300 feet to areas only a few feet above sea level.

Slanting toward the edge of the sea, the Coastal Plain runs flat except for a series of terraces descending to the coast. Scarps such as the one near Orangeburg mark each terrace. The Orangeburg scarp, produced by a transient shoreline, rises 250 feet above sea level.

Blackwater and brownwater rivers break up the rolling hills of the Upper Coastal Plain, and once again the familiar refrain of available moisture in the soil determines to a major extent vegetal communities present.

Mixed hardwoods and pine dominate the forests with loblolly pine reigning over other pines. Post oak, southern red oak, mockernut hickory and pignut hickory constitute the common hardwoods in dry forests.

❧December Moon (facing page)
Bare, winter limbs fashion a latticework across a full moon along the Wateree. Changing seasons and moon cycles affect nature's rhythms.
Twilight in December in Sumter County.
F 8, 1/2 Second, 600mm, Kodachrome 64

❧Pink Meadow Beauties (facing page)
Pink meadow beauties festoon the base of a pond cypress tree in a Carolina bay. Like many plants and animals occurring in the temporary wetlands of bays, these adaptable wildflowers conform to the cycle of filling and drying. Rain and runoff fill the bays—the summer sun drys them.
Early morning in July in Sumter County. F 22, 1/8 Second, 35mm, Kodachrome 25

❧Cypress Knees and Buttresses
Tree-borne watermarks trace flood levels along the Wateree River. Periodic flooding places rigors on trees, and the cypress knees and swollen trunks or buttresses may be adaptions to the soggy, unstable floodplain soil.
Late afternoon in October in Richland County. F 22, 1/15 Second, 55mm, Kodachrome 64

In the moist forests, white oak prevails with sweetgum, beech, and southern sugar maple playing back-up roles. Dogwood, hollies, sourwood and ti-ti fill the understory.

Standing over the rivers, bluffs distinguish the Upper Coastal Plain featuring abundant beech trees, a prolific understory and a herbaceous layer offering beechdrops, Indian pipe, heartleaf, crane-fly orchid and fern species.

Along the river edges lie the bottomland hardwood forests, floodplain forests and cypress-tupelo forests, habitats associated with large streams. Bald cypress and water tupelo tower above the

❧Loggerhead Shrike
The loggerhead shrike is a fierce predator in a small package known also as the butcher bird for its trait of impaling prey on thorns as storage for later consumption. These masked birds are most common in the Coastal Plain.
Late afternoon in November in Bamberg County. F 5.6, 1/500 Second, 600mm, Kodachrome 64

floodplain. As with all habitats, changing moisture levels bring about shifts in vegetation. Willow oak, laurel oak and swamp chestnut oak cast their shade along the rivers as do green ash, American elm, sycamore and cottonwood.

Hackberry, hollies, musclewood and swamp dogwood can be common in the understory, but like Piedmont floodplains, these dynamic habitats experience periodic flooding with the result that herbaceous plants may grow somewhat thinly.

One physiographic feature, in particular, adds distinction to the Upper Coastal Plain, and this feature occurs as a series of isolated freshwater wetlands: the Carolina Bays. Scattered across the

☙CAROLINA BAY SAND RIM
Turkey oaks and long-leaf pine reign supreme in the xeric habitat of a Carolina Bay's sand rim. Bordering the edges of a number of Carolina Bays, these sand deposits resemble the Fall Line Sandhills.
LATE AFTERNOON IN NOVEMBER IN CLARENDON COUNTY. F 22, 1/8 SECOND, 24MM WITH POLARIZING FILTER, KODACHROME 64

The Coastal Plain ☙ 71

❧ Venus' Flytrap
A plant wonder, the Venus' Flytrap, grows only in ecotonal habitats (areas of transition) between distinct habitat types in the Carolinas. Damp, sandy soils between pocosin habitats and sand rims of Carolina Bays grow this carnivorous plant.
Midmorning in June in Horry County.   F 22, 1/2 Second, 105mm, Kodachrome 25

RED-FRINGED PITCHER PLANTS
Raindrops from a recent thunderstorm glisten on red-fringed yellow pitcher plants, so-named for their flowers. Mingling with the ferns, the pitcher plants create a fairy tale landscape in a coastal plain savanna.
MIDMORNING IN JUNE IN BERKELEY COUNTY.   F 16, 1/2 SECOND, 35MM, KODACHROME 64

Coastal Plain these shallow, oval-shaped depressions feature abundant, diverse species of vegetation and a cast of wildlife species to match.

Many bays cover a few dozen acres; some occupy a thousand acres or more. All possess long axes pointing from northwest to southeast.

These elliptical basins collect rainwater and hold it perched slightly above the normal water table. Thus, it's not surprising that most bays feature a preponderance of wet habitat, quagmires— perhaps a shallow lake. Many bays possess a grassy savanna. With such a diversity of habitat packed into a compact area, life flourishes, and Carolina Bays are tantamount to zoological and botanical museums scattered across the Coastal Plain.

Some have sand rims, but most do not. The sand rims that do occur are not only striking, they also bring an end to the bay's wetland habitat, and turkey oaks and long-leaf pine sprout from the sand, a sharp contrast to the verdant cypress in wetter areas.

A fairly typical bay supports quite a diverseness of wild vegetation: pitcher plants, bladderworts, lush grasses, yellow jessamine, clinging vines, ubiquitous waterlilies and, of course, bay trees from whence the name Carolina Bays comes. Shallow areas of black water nurture pocosins (shrub bogs) adding still more diversity to the Carolina Bay's already well-rounded character.

Pond cypress and black gum, of course, are a major part of a bay's identity. Wet meadows bring splotches of green to some of the elliptical wetlands, a green that can come and go as most bays fill and dry with the rain cycle.

❧ SPOTTED SALAMANDER
The spotted salamander of the mole salamander family inhabits woodlands near wetlands and small, sluggish streams. In the winter, adults migrate to wetlands to lay eggs and then return to land. Their aquatic larvae remain in the wetland until early spring brings metamorphosis.
MORNING IN JUNE IN BERKELEY COUNTY.
F 22, 1/15 SECOND, 55MM, KODACHROME 64

❧ SILHOUETTES OF VULTURES (facing page)
The stately forms of black vultures on an oak snag cut silhouettes against the dawn sky. By feeding on carrion and decaying matter, these scavengers occupy yet another vital niche in nature's time-perfected scheme.
DAWN IN NOVEMBER IN HAMPTON COUNTY.
F 5.6, 1/30 SECOND, 600MM, KODACHROME 64

Some—very few—are spring fed. And the presence of water is, naturally, a determinant of what does or does not grow in a bay.

The multifaceted character of Carolina Bays steeps the Upper Coastal Plain with a legion of wildlife. Wild creatures carry out the drama of life within and around a bay's confines. Waterfowl, especially woodduck, seek refuge in the cypress-studded blackwater.

Bobcats prowl swampy recesses. Squirrels chatter high above the mirrored waters, and, egrets, of course, cast shards of white against the bay's dark interior.

In the more open waters, patrolling alligators resembling partially sunken logs slide through channels.

There is no doubt that Carolina Bays are the dominant, isolated freshwater feature of South Carolina.

The wildlife of the Upper Coastal Plain truly paints a dynamic portrait. Wild turkey feed on acorns in forests that slope down ridges to bottomlands. Red-shouldered hawks glide over the forests, their acute vision scanning the woods for favored prey such as field mice and an occasional squirrel.

The haunting calls of barred owls reverberate through the recesses of bottomland hardwood forests. The yellow-bellied turtle (also known as sliders or cooters and probably the most common freshwater turtle) suns atop the logs floating in ponds, sloughs, and the backwaters of streams and rivers. The merest hint of danger and they slide into the black water.

Amphibian species such as the barking tree frog, ornate chorus frog, mole salamander, and tiger salamander find the Carolina Bays to be important breeding sites.

A balmy spring evening in a Carolina Bay comes alive with choruses of frogs, punctuated by the deep bass of the dominant frog, the bullfrog. As wildlife concerts go, it has no equal. And the same can be said about the natural diversity of South Carolina's Upper Coastal Plain. Were the Carolina Bays nonexistent, the Upper Coastal Plain would nonetheless continue to be blessed with a superlative assemblage of natural habitats: river bottoms, oxbows, savannas, swamps and river bluffs.

It is an extraordinary land, this great plain that once lay beneath ancient, ever-changing oceans.

꙳MAPLE LEAVES ON WATER
Red maple leaves float on still backwaters of the Edisto. As the leaves decompose, light brown tannins will leach into the river imbuing it with the color of tea. Canopy trees of the floodplain forest reflect off the dark, mirrorlike water.
LATE AFTERNOON IN NOVEMBER IN COLLETON COUNTY. F 16, 8 SECONDS, 35MM, KODACHROME 64

The Coastal Zone

The land meets the sea here. Witness to this confrontation are the sea islands, marshlands, tidal reaches and estuaries. The shifting nature of sand and water creates a soft edge curving in and out nearly 185 miles. Inlets interrupt the great arc of the northern Coastal Zone.

The Santee Delta, with its huge outlay of sedimentary deposits, provides a gentle, round promontory breaking the coast's southward sweep. The Coastal

❧ Sea Oats
Sea oats, that familiar large grass restricted to foredunes, stabilizes otherwise shifting sands. Anchoring the sand with its root system, sea oats helps maintain the sand dunes as the first line of defense against an encroaching sea.
Late afternoon in September in Beaufort County.   F 11, 1/30 Second, 200mm with Polarizing Filter, Kodachrome 25

ᴥMARSH AERIAL
Vast expanses of spartina marsh blanket South Carolina's Coastal Zone, and decomposing spartina grass forms the basis for the estuarine food chain. Incoming and outgoing tides cycle nutrients through the arterial drainage system, giving fishes, crabs, shrimp and other organisms highly productive nursery grounds.
LATE AFTERNOON IN NOVEMBER IN GEORGETOWN COUNTY.   F 4, 1/500 SECOND, 55MM, KODACHROME 64

❧Wind Patterns in Sand (facing page)
Wind etches intricate patterns in the crest of a foredune where heavier particles of garnet gather to create near topographic designs against the lighter shades of silicate—a motif seen throughout the dunes.
Early morning in September in Charleston County.
F 16, 1/15 Second, 105mm, Kodachrome 25

❧Maritime Forest
The maritime forest where dominating live oaks, laurel oak and magnolia border the marsh. Salt-laden spray sculpts the trees, and many succumb to the elements as evidenced by their bleached skeletons.
Late afternoon in September in Charleston County. F 11, 1/60 Second, 300mm, Kodachrome 64

The Coastal Plain ❧ 81

🍀PINE FLATWOODS
A thin pine canopy discloses a flatwoods community. Maintained by periodic wildfires, these habitats harbor a wealth of showy wildflowers and rare animals such as red-cockaded woodpeckers and flatwoods salamanders.
MIDMORNING IN NOVEMBER IN CHARLESTON COUNTY. F 16, 1/30 SECOND, 24MM WITH POLARIZING FILTER, KODACHROME 64

Zone reaches inland about ten miles.

Within the inland reach of the Coastal Zone, forests dominate the landscape. Swamps flow out of the Coastal Zone rivers where magnificent stands of forests reach skyward. The dark reaches of these swamps feature a dense canopy, and cathedral-like vaults of bald cypress and hardwoods shut out the bright coastal sun.

Not too far away, sunlight splatters upland forests where mixed pine and hardwoods sprout. Pine flatwoods featuring long-leaf pine and loblolly pine stretch parallel to the lower coast, and these dry forests feature open canopies where even more sunlight penetrates. Grasses, sedges and wildflower species dwell in profusion.

In the moister areas, pine or pond cypress savannas feature still sparser canopies. Here, occur pitcher plants, orchids and sprays of wildflowers. Further south, the slash pine-saw palmetto flatwoods exist. The flatwoods and savanna communities would undergo plant succession were it not for periodic fires which rid their understory of hardwood species which, sooner or later, would dominate them.

In contrast to the piney flatlands and savannas is the maritime forest, a fringe of forest bordering estuarine areas. Here grow picturesque, wind-shaped trees: live oak, laurel oak, magnolia, loblolly and slash pines. Beneath their canopies, cabbage palmetto, wax myrtle, red bay and red cedar fill the understory. Maritime forests flaunt their unique niche on the mainland, on occasional hammocks and on some of the larger barrier islands.

Perhaps the habitat most closely identified with the Coastal Zone is the estuary. Though the Coastal Zone is a narrow corridor lying alongside the Atlantic, its green-fringed, water-laced expanse forms more than one million acres of land and water. Much of this is the estuary.

The Coastal Zone's carpet of marshland begins as rivers enter it from the Upper Coastal Plain. Rivers entering the estuarine reaches broaden and vast areas of marsh flourish. This is true, especially, in the southern end of the Coastal Zone with its wider fresh and brackish water marshes. Coursing seaward, the rivers encounter tidal surges, producing a brackish region where fresh and saltwater intermingle, providing a transition to the saltwater marshes. The intricate reaches and tidal nooks and crannies stretch for several thousand miles.

This labyrinthine maze of marshes provides some of the richest, most productive habitat known on the face of the Earth. Salt marsh, dominated by spartina, otherwise known as smooth cordgrass, provides a fertile region that lays down the basis for the estuarine food chain. Other species such as needle rush and the salt flats with saltwort, baccharis and other salt-tolerant species add to the diversity of this watery region.

Nothing is quite so beautiful as the wind rippling through a sunny salt marsh. Whitecaps fleck the blue-green water, and here and there a bank of oyster shells breaks up the line where water meets marsh. A solitary egret stands stark against a thick clump of green cord

ˇ♣Lowcountry Maples
As autumn light shuts down the production of chlorophyll, the green veins of red maples betray areas where the last traces of pigment known for photosynthesis linger.
Early morning in November in Georgetown County. F 16, 1/8 Second, 55mm, Kodachrome 64

The Coastal Plain ˇ♣ 83

grass, while the great blue heron, large though it is, blends well with the edge of water meeting the distant blue horizon.

Beneath the water, blue crabs scurry about. Shrimp, fish and a host of other species move in congress about the estuary. Periwinkles climb the stalks of marsh grass. Black pluff mud awaits the next inundation of high tide. The raucous cry of gulls fills the air, and a bevy of shorebirds descend to feed on the natural litter left by the out-going tide. The fertile smell of a saltmarsh . . . it's the aroma of life.

Another region dynamic with life and geologic processes stands close by— the shore. Compared to the Mountain Province, the Piedmont and even the Sandhills, the area where land meets the water is new. Geologic actions continue to shape this unstable region, in particular, the force of erosion. Wind and wave action form beaches on land directly facing the sea. The wind piles up great heaps of sand, and rows of sand dunes softly undulate parallel to the surfline.

While the dune system serves as a buffer against an encroaching sea, coastal erosion continues to claim new land. The craggy remains of stumps testify to the force of moving water and shifting sand. Maritime forests slip ever

❧WHITE-TAILED DEER
Ever alert, this deer relies on sharp senses of smell, hearing and sight as it travels down a well-worn trail.
EARLY MORNING IN DECEMBER IN GEORGETOWN COUNTY. F 5.6, 400MM, 1/250 SECOND, KODACHROME 64

❧SANTEE DELTA SUNRISE (facing page)
A winter sun climbs quickly through the dawn. Rays of light flood the spartina marshes setting the miracle of photosynthesis into action. A salt marsh may well be one of the Earth's most productive habitats . . . And like everything else in nature, it all begins with sunlight.
SUNRISE IN NOVEMBER IN GEORGETOWN COUNTY. F 8, 1/125 SECOND, 400MM, KODACHROME 64

ꙮLOGGERHEAD TURTLES
Hatchling loggerheads begin an arduous journey that will take them through great risks. Leaving their nest site on the upper reaches of a sandy beach, the young turtles head for the surfline. Tracks in the sand attest to the passage of their fellow hatchlings before them.
EARLY MORNING IN SEPTEMBER IN GEORGETOWN COUNTY.   F 8, 1/30 SECOND, 55MM, KODACHROME 64

ꙮGREAT BLUE HERON (facing page)
Frozen amidst the green stalks of cattails, a great blue heron scans a freshwater slough for the telltale movement of a fish. These large wading birds, common in South Carolina, feed in fresh, brackish or saltwater.
LATE AFTERNOON IN NOVEMBER IN JASPER COUNTY. F 5.6, 1/500 SECOND, 600MM, KODACHROME 64

so gradually beneath the sea. And the advent of a northeaster drives home the point that this is, indeed, a land subject to the whims of nature.

Geologically, the Coastal Zone is young. The barrier islands along the coast, for instance, were nonexistent several thousand years ago. Seawater ranged farther inland, and sweeps of saltwater covered the present-day coast. Then the shoreline inched west, pausing now and then, building dune ridges along beaches, then leaving them.

When the Ice Age ended, the sea re-

INTERDUNAL WILDFLOWERS
The delicate pink blossoms of Seashore Mallow, a perennial herb related to other native mallows and hibiscus, brings color to an interdunal marsh during autumn.
EARLY MORNING IN SEPTEMBER IN CHARLESTON COUNTY.
F 11, 1/8 SECOND, 105MM, KODACHROME 64

turned to inundate a part of the land it once claimed, isolating older dune ridges from the mainland in the process. The sea parted around them, leaving them as islands. Barrier islands then became a part of the state's diverse habitat. South Carolina's barrier islands signify the edge of the North American continent.

The sea island section, featuring inlets and bays, possesses two types of barrier islands: active barrier islands and remnant islands, islands once a part of the mainland but long since cutoff by

BLACK SKIMMER CHICKS
Two black skimmer chicks huddle on the sand. Like many shorebirds, the nests of black skimmers are merely scrapes in the shell debris of small sandbar islands. As adults, they will fly with their lower bill skimming the water to catch small fish, a feeding mechanism unique among birds.
TWILIGHT IN EARLY JULY IN GEORGETOWN COUNTY.   F 4, 1/60 SECOND, 105MM, KODACHROME 64

erosion and then surrounded by the Ice Age's advancing waters.

Both on the front head of barrier islands and the shore exist magnificent dune systems. Between the tall, soft mounds of sand and open beach may exist interdunal pools, grasslands and shrub thickets. Foredunes festooned with sea oats stand guard over the Atlantic.

The power, ever-changing ways, and vibrancy of nature are manifest where land and water confront each other.

The Coastal Zone is a mosaic full of grandeur—rolling breakers, moss-laden oaks, and salt marshes flecked white with egrets. Shorebirds swirl above rookeries where sand scrapes are all the nests they need.

ಜೆCabbage Palmetto
Possessing an association with the coast equal to sea oats, the slender trunk and waving fronds of the cabbage palmetto lend a tropical aura to the shore. A fallen cabbage palmetto may lie upon the beach for decades as its wood is extremely resistant to decay.
Early morning in early June in Charleston County. F 22, 1/15 Second, 50mm, Fuji 50, 2.25 Format

ಜೆFlight of Pelicans (facing page)
The red glow of sunrise breaks through morning clouds onto a barrier island as Eastern brown pelicans skim small breakers in quest of menhaden and other small, schooling fish.
Morning in June in Charleston County. F 8, 1/125 Second, 200mm, Kodachrome 64

☙Tidal Pool Shells
Reflections of the coast. Light passing through a shallow tidal pool shimmers into patterns as a thin layer of seawater magnifies water-washed jewels of the sea.
Late afternoon in June in Charleston County.   F 8, 1/125 Second, 105mm, Kodachrome 64

Nearby a wedge of eastern brown pelicans rides the wind as they head out for a morning of fishing.

Wading birds frequent the freshwater ponds of the barrier islands. White-tailed deer approach the margins to sip, while kingfishers perched upon snags call, making their presence known. Raccoons prowl the shallow edges.

And all of this dynamic life exists, in a sense, as an oasis, a pool of freshwater within a small land engulfed by saltwater.

From June to mid-August, the giant loggerhead sea turtles crawl up the gentle slopes of barrier islands and beaches to lay their clutches against the dunes.

Osprey hunt for fish over estuaries and creeks. Herons, egrets, and ibis feed along shallow coastal waters, tidal marshes and creeks.

Alligators haul out to sun along the banks of coastal, brackish or freshwater rivers.

Eastern diamondback rattlesnakes slide along the ridges of pine flatwoods and barrier islands.

The rare shortnose sturgeon and the striped bass, both anadromous fish, migrate from the sea up freshwater rivers to spawn.

And the great bald eagle soars over the land, a majestic species, head flashing white in the bright Carolina sun.

South Carolina's edge where land meets the sea is a magnificent land.

☙Maritime Sunrise (facing page)
Coastal erosion is an on-going process. Encroaching upon the maritime forest at the northern end of a barrier island, the sea topples trees onto the sand; at the island's southern end, sand accumulates, in effect, moving the island southward.
Dawn in late November in Charleston County.
F 16, 1 Second, 80mm, Fuji 50,
2.25 Format

Epilogue

Many of the habitats and special places you have just visited exist in South Carolina today only as remnants or fragments of once widespread communities. You have just visited a South Carolina untainted, unchanged by the hands of man, a South Carolina that does not exist today.

We consciously, deliberately chose to present a picture of the state which excluded man. Now we must bring him—us—back into that picture.

There is a philosophical question facing those concerned with the environment. Some would contend that man, a species which evolved on the face of the Earth, is part of the natural scheme. And therefore, any changes wrought by man's hands are natural changes.

On the other hand, some might contend that man has come so far in his development of technology, that he has uncoupled himself from the natural world.

We do not hold the answer to this argument. We do, however, know that whether you consider man's influence to be natural or not, it is completely reshaping the planet.

We have changed South Carolina forever. Rich bottomland forests have been logged or converted to agriculture. In the United States, 80 percent of this once widespread community has been lost. And along with it, we have lost the ivory-billed woodpecker, a species which required large tracts of bottomland forest for its survival.

The once widespread hardwood forests of the Piedmont were razed to grow cotton leaving Piedmont soils barren of nutrients. Poor farming practices resulted in tremendous erosion leaving the land rutted and gullied. Where ancient forests of hickory, oak and shortleaf pine once reigned, monocultures of loblolly pine and shortleaf pine are lucky to reach thirty years of age before being harvested. Stories such as these can be told all across South Carolina.

Man's survival in South Carolina has depended upon the products of environmental changes. We must have the produce, fiber and timber products land provides. We require the power generated by hydroelectric dams. We are the cause of urban sprawl, overdeveloped beaches and pollution.

As change was wrought on the land in the name of survival and progress, our forests slipped away. The widespread habitats constricted; the uncommon became rare; the rare vanished or teetered on the brink.

Just as everything pictured in this book is connected, entwined with every other thing, so are we undeniably linked to our environment, our habitat. Every action we take in the name of survival or progress ripples through the natural world.

The scenes in this book are forever frozen in time. They will not change. The real world is trapped in a continuum of change, and we are the major source of that change.

Our choices are difficult ones. The world is complex, and many times we lack sufficient information to make the right decision. Perhaps our images of South Carolina are all the information we need. Preserving for future generations as much of our remaining natural wealth as possible is not just the right decision; it is the only decision.

Future South Carolinians may forgive us many things, but they surely could not, nor should we expect them to, forgive us if images such as those in our book are the sole remnants of the once-great natural heritage they inherit from our generation.

Stephen H. Bennett

Robert C. Clark

Thomas M. Poland

❧ Photographer's Comments

Many photographers are in a constant search for spectacular photographs. Many of them pass by South Carolina in quest of unique images. To photograph South Carolina is a lesson in the sublime.

The diversity of this state is tremendous. Just moving several feet horizontally can yield different subjects. Many close-ups exist in this book because South Carolina presents a palette of intimate portraits. All you need to do is see beyond the vistas so popular in contemporary photography.

Finally, I urge each person living in South Carolina to save what little precious, unspoiled lands remain. That is the key to preserving the natural treasures found within South Carolina.

❧Bibliography

Barry, John M. 1980. *Natural Vegetation of South Carolina.* Columbia, S.C.; University of South Carolina Press.

Bell, Henry III., J. Robert Butler, David E. Howell, and Walter H. Wheeler. 1974. *Geology of the Piedmont and Coastal Plain Near Pageland, South Carolina and Wadesboro, North Carolina.* U.S. Geological Survey, Department of the Interior.

Kovacik, Charles F., and John J. Winberry. 1987. *South Carolina: A Geography.* Boulder, Co.: Westview Press.

Nelson, John B. 1986 *The Natural Communities of South Carolina: Initial Classification and Description.* A Report of the Nongame and Heritage Trust Section of the South Carolina Wildlife and Marine Resources Department.

Nystrom, Paul G. Jr., Ralph H. Willoughby, and Lucille E. Kite. 1986. *Cretaceous-Tertiary Stratigraphy of the Upper Edge of the Coastal Plain Between North Augusta and Lexington, South Carolina.* Columbia, S.C.: Carolina Geological Survey: Field Trip Guidebook.

Overstreet, W.C., and Henry Bell III. 1965. *Geologic Map of the Crystalline Rocks of South Carolina.* U.S. Geological Survey, Department of the Interior.

Radford, Albert E., Harry E. Ahles, and C. Ritchie Bell. 1964. *Manual of the Vascular Flora of the Carolinas.* Chapel Hill, N.C.: University of North Carolina Press.

Snoke, Arthur W., editor. 1978. *Geological Investigations of the Eastern Piedmont, Southern Appalachians.* West Columbia, S.C.: Carolina Geological Society: Fieldtrip Guidebook.

Savage, Henry. 1982. *The Mysterious Carolina Bays.* Columbia, S.C.: University of South Carolina Press.